CHRONICLE OF A
DEATH FORETOLD

Gabriel Garcia Marquez

AUTHORED by Hannah Wallace
UPDATED AND REVISED by W.C. Miller

COVER DESIGN by Table XI Partners LLC
COVER PHOTO by Olivia Verma and © 2005 GradeSaver, LLC

BOOK DESIGN by Table XI Partners LLC

Published by GradeSaver LLC, www.gradesaver.com

First published in the United States of America by GradeSaver LLC. 2006

GRADESAVER, the GradeSaver logo and the phrase "Getting you the grade since 1999" are registered trademarks of GradeSaver, LLC

ISBN 978–1–60259–014–4

Printed in the United States of America

For other products and additional information please visit
http://www.gradesaver.com

Table of Contents

Biography of Gabriel Garcia Marquez (1928–)...1

About Chronicle of a Death Foretold..5

Character List..7

Major Themes...11

Glossary of Terms...15

Short Summary...17

Summary and Analysis of Chapter 1...19
    Summary..19
    Analysis...20

Summary and Analysis of Chapter 2...23
    Summary..23
    Analysis...24

Summary and Analysis of Chapter 3...27
    Summary..27
    Analysis...28

Summary and Analysis of Chapter 4...31
    Summary..31
    Analysis...32

Summary and Analysis of Chapter 5...35
    Summary..35
    Analysis...36

Suggested Essay Questions..39

The Boom: Latin American Literature in the mid to late 1900s........................41

Author of ClassicNote and Sources..43

Essay: Honor Codes and Ritual Contrition..45

Quiz 1...49

Table of Contents

Quiz 1 Answer Key...55

Quiz 2...57

Quiz 2 Answer Key...63

Quiz 3...65

Quiz 3 Answer Key...71

Quiz 4...73

Quiz 4 Answer Key...79

Biography of Gabriel Garcia Marquez (1928–)

Gabriel Jose Garcia Marquez was born on March 6, 1928 to Luisa Santiaga Marquez Iguaran and Gabriel Eligio Garcia in Aracataca, Colombia. The prized author and journalist is known to many as simply Gabo. With lyricism and marked wisdom, Marquez has been recognized as one of the most remarkable storytellers of the 20th Century.

Luisa's parents did not approve of her marriage to Gabriel and Marquez, the oldest of twelve children, was sent to live with his maternal grandparents. On December 6, in the Cienaga train station, between 9 and 3,000 striking banana workers were shot and killed by troops from Antioquia. The incident was officially forgotten and omitted from Colombian history textbooks. Although Marquez was still a baby, this event was to have a profound effect on his writing.

When Marquez was eight years old, his grandfather died. At that time it was also clear that his grandmother, who was going blind, was increasingly helpless. He was sent to live with his parents and siblings, who he barely knew, in Sucre. A bright pupil, he won scholarships to complete his secondary education at the Colegio Nacional. There he discovered literature and admired a group of poets called the piedra y cielo ("stone and sky"). This group included Eduardo Carranza, Jorge Rojas, and Aurelio Arturo and their literary grandfathers were Juan Ramon Jimenez and Pablo Neruda. In 1946, Marquez entered law school at the National University of Bogota. There he began reading Kafka and publishing his first short stories in leading Liberal newspapers.

Marquez's literary career was sparked, oddly enough, by the long period of political violence and repression known in Colombia as la violencia. On April 9, 1948, the assassination of the Liberal presidential candidate led to three days of riots. One of the buildings that burned was Marquez's pension, and his manuscripts were destroyed along with his living quarters. The National University was closed and Marquez was forced to go to the university in Cartagena and take up journalism to support himself. In 1950 he abandoned his legal studies and began writing columns and stories for El Heraldo, a Liberal newspaper. He also began associating with a group of young writers in the area, who admired modernists like Joyce, Woolf and Hemingway and introduced Marquez to Faulkner. In 1954 he returned to Bogota, as a reporter for El Espectador.

Marquez's first novel Leaf Storm was published by a small Bogota press in 1955. That same year he began attending meetings of the Colombian Communist Party and traveling to Europe as a foreign correspondent. He also wrote his second novel, In Evil Hour, and began work on a collection of short stories called No one Writes to the Colonel. In 1956, Marquez was in Paris as a correspondent for El Espectador when he learned that the dictator Rojas Pinalla had closed the newspaper. Stuck in

France, Marquez cashed in his return plane ticket, went hunting for journalism work, and collected bottles to help pay the cost of his rent. The next year he managed to travel in Eastern Europe and secure an editor position at a newspaper in Caracas. In 1958 he returned to Barranquilla to marry Mercedes Barcha. (He claimed that she was 13 when he first proposed.)

On January 1, 1959, Fidel Castro's guerrilla revolution triumphed and the fighters marched into Havana. This revolution was of crucial importance to contemporary Latin American history and its impact on Marquez cannot be overstated. That same year he became the Bogota correspondent for Prensa Latina, the new Cuban news agency. Also of note (and this becomes of importance in One Hundred Years of Solitude) is the birth of his first child, Rodrigo, that year on August 24. Marquez spent the next two years in the United States, working for Prensa Latina. In 1961 he won the Esso Literary Prize in Colombia for In Evil Hour. When the book was republished in Madrid a year later with unauthorized language changes, he repudiated the edition.

For four years, Marquez wrote no new fiction and was subject to derision for his writer's block. Instead, he concentrated on raising his family (his son Gonzalo was born in April 1962) and writing screenplays, one of them with the famed Mexican writer Carlos Fuentes. In January 1965, his writer's block broke on a family trip to Acapulco. He turned the car around, drove back to the home they were staying at in Mexico, and barricaded himself there for, as he claims, "15 months." When he emerged, the 1967 book One Hundred Years of Solitude was immediately hailed as a classic. It was an incredible popular success as well and at one point it was selling out an edition every week. It was published in English in 1970 and won many prizes in different countries.

In 1973, following the assassination of Chile's president Salvador Allende, Marquez decided to take a more active political role. He founded a left–wing magazine, Alternativa, in Bogota and participated in the Russell Tribunal to publicize human rights abuses in Latin America. In 1975, he published The Autumn of the Patriarch and traveled frequently to Havana, where he prepared a book on Cuban life under the U.S. blockade. He also established personal relationships with Fidel Castro and the Pananamanian dictator Omar Torrijos, and in 1978, established a human rights organization in Mexico City.

Three important events happened for Marquez in 1981. He was awarded the French Legion of Honor, the highest decoration France gives to a foreigner. After a warning that the Colombian military had accused him of conspiring with guerrillas, he was forced to seek asylum at the Mexican Embassy in Bogota. Finally, he published Chronicle of a Death Foretold. In 1982, he won the Nobel Prize for Literature. He used the money to start a daily newspaper, El Otro, in Colombia, after the Colombian government promised him that he would be safe in Colombia.

In the 1980s and 1990s, Marquez lived in Mexico City and Colombia. He continued to take an active role in politics and organization and in 1986 he organized the Foundation of New Latin American Cinema in Havana. He also wrote screenplays, plays, and two novels: Love in the Time of Cholera (1985) and The General in his Labyrinth (1989). As the century closed he continued to live in Colombia and write, although under heavy security for fear of kidnapping or other crimes with which he has been threatened.

Gabriel Garcia Marquez has many trademarks in his novels. For instance, both Chronicle of a Death Foretold and One Hundred Years of Solitude start out in media res, or in the middle of things, with a declaration that their protagonists are going to die in the novel. Also, Marquez often uses parts and characters of his own life in his books. For example, Mercedes Barcha, his wife, is in Chronicle of a Death Foretold under her own name, as the narrator's young wife. The narrator even says he proposed to her as soon as she finished primary school, much like the real–life Mercedes Barcha, who Marquez proposed to at the age of 13. Luisa Santiaga is both the narrator's mother in the book, and Marquez's mother's name in real life. Marquez's brother is named Luis Enrique; both the narrator and Marquez have a sister who is a nun.

Gabriel Garcia Marquez is still living, but suffers from lymphatic cancer. He is currently receiving treatment for the cancer.

Biography of Gabriel Garcia Marquez (1928–)

About Chronicle of a Death Foretold

Gabriel Garcia Marquez's novel, *Chronicle of a Death Foretold*, is a hybrid of literary genres, at once a journalistic account of a historical murder that took place in Sucre, Columbia, a psychological detective story, and a work of allegorical fiction. On January 22, 1951, two brothers in the Chica family murdered Cayetano Gentile Chimento, because he has sex with their sister, Margarita Chica Salas, before her marriage to Miguel Reyes Palencia. When Miguel discovered her lack of virginity, he returned Margarita to the Chica Salas family, at which point they discovered and killed the man who had deflowered her. This historical murder provides the provides the main thrust of the story in *Chronicle of a Death Foretold*; the work is not pure history, however, in that it stages the murder in a narrative fashion and takes several fictional liberties in telling the story. Moreover, Garcia Marquez is less concerned with the recording of facts (the specific historical setting of the novel, for instance, is never mentioned, and the names in the novel have been changed) than he is with an exploration of the murderers' reasons for going through with the murder, as well as the townsfolk's reasons for allowing the murder to happen against their collective conscience. The result is quite unique and striking—a balance of journalism and allegory, of history and morality play.

Each generic component of *Chronicle of a Death Foretold* is expressed stylistically. The journalistic concern comes through both in Garcia Marquez' detached consideration of the daily habits of the denizens of the town as well as in a strict time line. The novel is calibrated down to the minute. We know that Santiago woke up at 5:30 in the morning to see the bishop, and that he was dead by 7:05. To put Garcia Marquez' style in flatly journalistic terms, he is always concerned with showing us the *who, where, when and how.*

He is also concerned with the *why,* which comprises the psychological component of the story. As the title suggests, there is no mystery surrounding the death of Santiago Nasar, the character based on the historical Cayetano. We know that he is killed, when he is killed and who killed him immediately. But the *why* of his death—the complex social milieu that both tolerates and despises the murder—is not so clear. Marquez dispassionately (more or less) presents the social pressures at work, allowing us not a simple answer or a simple judgment but merely a glimpse into the welter of justice and injustice foregrounded by Santiago and Angela's alleged tryst.

Finally, the story works on the level of allegory, using a variety of biblical references to comment upon the morality or immorality of Santiago's death. Garcia Marquez regularly paints Santiago as a Christ–like character. Santiago appears with a stigmata–like stab wound on his hand, for instance, and is murdered wearing a white linen suit, which summons images of Biblical robes and of sacrificial lambs, suggesting Santiago's ultimate innocence. Moreover, Santiago is impaled on a wooden door, like Christ to the cross, in broad daylight with a crowd of people watching: a public crucifixion of sorts.

The novel was published in 1981. In allowing its publication Garcia Marquez broke a self–imposed "publication strike," under which, for years, he had refused to publish any work until the Chilean dictator, Augusto Pinochet, was no longer in power. *Chronicle of a Death Foretold* was an immediate success; more than a million copies of the novel were printed in its initial publishing run. Marquez won the Nobel Prize in literature in 1982, the following year.

Character List

Santiago Nasar

the protagonist of the story who is killed the day after the wedding between Angela Vicario and Bayardo San Roman. The story is centered around his death and the events leading up to it. He is accused by Angela Vicario of taking her virinity, but no evidence backs this up.

Angela Vicario

the bride of Bayardo San Roman, who accuses Santiago Nasar of taking her virginity. After being returned home on her wedding night, she discovers that she's in love with Bayardo, and, later on, begins sending him one letter a week for 17 years.

Pedro Vicario

one of Angela's twin brothers. He was in the army before the time the novel is set, and after prison he reenlisted and eventually disappeared in enemy territory. Pedro originally came up with the plan to kill Santiago Nasar, but after the mayor, Colonel Aponte, disarmed them and sent them home, he was ready to give up on the plan.

Pablo Vicario

the older twin by six minutes, he developed a sort of younger–brother complex after Pedro returned form the army. Pablo was the one who took command after Pedro wanted to stop the murder plot. He marries Prudencia Cotes after he is acquitted of the murder and released from prison.

Bayardo SanRoman

the mysterious man who marries Angela Vicario and then returns her when he discovers that she wasn't a virgin. Bayardo is the son of General Petronio San Roman, a famous civil war general, and Alberta Simonds, who many considered the most beautiful woman in the Antilles. The family is extremely wealthy, and Bayardo came to town with the sole purpose of finding a bride.

Placida Linero

Santiago Nasar's mother. She is well–known in the town for being adept at interpreting people's dreams, but failed to notice the bad omen of birds in Santiago Nasar's in the days before his death.

Purisma del Carmen

more often referred to as Pura Vicario, she is Angela's mother. She beats Angela for two hours when Bayardo returns her to the family house. She is a blood relative of the narrator's.

Poncio Vicario

Angela Vicario's father. He is blind, a result of his working as a goldsmith.

Maria Alejandrina Cervantes

A local and well–respected prostitute, she is a good friend of both the narrator's and Santiago Nasar.

Ibrahim Nasar

Santiago's father who came over with the other Arab immigrants and died before the story began. Santiago is said to be a lot like his father.

Victoria Guzman

a servant in the Nasar household. She was seduced at a young age by Ibrahim Nasar, and is worried that her daughter, Divina Flor, will fall into the same problem with Santiago.

Clotilde Armenta

the proprietress of the milk shop that Pedro and Pablo Vicario wait in before killing Santiago. She tries to warn Santiago of the danger, by telling a number of different people to warn him, his mother, the local priest, and the mayor, but all of her attempts fail.

Don Rogelio de la Flor

Clotilde Armenta's husband who doesn't believe her that the Vicario brothers are actually planning on killing Santiago. He dies of shock (probably a heart attack) after watching the murder.

Divina Flor

the daughter of Victoria Guzman. Santiago grabs her "whole pussy" as he leaves; her mother is afraid that she'll fall under his trap like she did with his father.

Cristo Bedoya

one of Santiago's best friends. He spent all night and morning with Santiago, and then tried to warn him once he found out about the murder plot, but couldn't find him. He's also a good friend of the narrator.

Luis Enrique

the narrator's brother, who partied at Maria Cervantes's brothel and then serenaded with the narrator, Santiago Nasar, and Cristo Bedoya. Supposedly, Pedro and Pablo Vicario told them their plan to kill Santiago, but he was too drunk to remember.

Margot

the narrator's sister, who invites Santiago to breakfast the morning of his murder. She seems to have a crush on Santiago, and thinks that Flora Miguel is a very lucky woman.

Father Amador

the local priest, who is warned about the murder plot by Clothilde Armenta, but then forgets in the panic of the bishop's visit. He also performs the autopsy while the doctor is out of town.

Dr. Dionisio Iguaran

the local doctor, who would have performed the autopsy had he been in town. He was present when Xius sold Bayardo San Roman his old house, and thinks that Xius died of a broken heart from selling it.

Colonel Lazaro Aponte

the mayor of the town. He takes away the first two knives that the twins have, and sends them home, but refuses to arrest them, so they come back. He also goes into the social club to check on dominoes night instead of finding Santiago and warning him about the murder plot.

Faustino Santos

a butcher friend of the Vicario brothers, who warns a local policeman of their plan.

Officer Leandro Pornoy

the officer that Faustino warned of the plan. He passes along the information to Colonel Aponte, the mayor.

General Petronio San Roman

Bayardo's father, who was a hero of the civil wars of the past century.

Alberta Simonds

Bayardo's mother. She's considered to be one of the prettiest women in the Antilles.

Prudencia Cotes

Pablo Vicario's fiancee and later, wife. She told the narrator that she wouldn't have married him if he hadn't acted like a man and killed Santiago.

Yamil Shaium

a friend of Ibrahim Nasar, who immigrated to the town with him. He tried to protect Santiago by warning Cristo Bedoya, but it was too late. He then led the group of Arabs that chased the Vicario twins into the church.

Flora Miguel

Santiago's fiancee who gives him back all of his letters that he wrote her when she hears about the murder plot. She believes that the Vicario brothers won't kill Santiago, but make him marry Angela to give back her honor.

Nahir Miguel

the wise–man of the village, and Flora's father. He offered Santiago refuge after realizing that Santiago had no idea why the twins wanted to kill him. He also offered Santiago the use of his rifle, but Santiago refused both.

Xius

the man who Bayardo San Roman bought their house from. Angela called his house the prettiest in the town, so Bayardo paid him way more money than it was worth. However, Xius died two months later, out of "tears bubbling in his heart" from having to sell his wife's old house.

Magistrate

the judge the investigated the murder. His name isn't known, just that he had a passion for literature, and that what bothered him most about the murder was the absolute lack of evidence that Santiago had, in fact, taken Angela's virginity.

Mercedes Barcha

the narrator's fiancee and, eventually, wife. He proposed to her at Bayardo and Angela's wedding festivities.

Indalecio Pardo

a friend of Santiago Nasar's. The Vicario twins essentially challenged him to warn Santiago, but he was too afraid when it came down to it.

Major Themes

No one in *Chronicle of a Death Foretold* is purely guilty; Marquez makes every character in the story a partial victim. Angela Vicario, though she names Santiago as her lover and thus condemns him, is a victim of the double standard between the genders in her society; she is persecuted for having premarital sex, returned to her family and beaten, whereas men are expected to go to brothels and have as much premarital sex as they want. She is required to name a lover, and name she could have given would have been a death sentence for that man. Bayardo San Roman is also a victim of deceit, as he married Angela under the pretext that she was a virgin. While we may think that Angela's virginity or lack thereof shouldn't concern him, Bayardo, as a product of his culture, cannot help but return her. Santiago Nasar is obviously a victim as well; he is killed for taking Angela's virginity, an act that he likely did not commit. Finally, the Vicario twins are also victims of societal expectations: they are bound by honor to try to kill the man whom Angela cites as her lover. If they hadn't made this attempt, they would have been seen as weak and unmanly. Prudencia Cotes, for instance, told the narrator that she wouldn't have married Pablo Vicario if he hadn't been a man and killed Santiago.

Just as Marquez gives all of his characters a measure of innocence in Santiago's death, so too he gives them a measure of guilt for the murder. Angela, clearly, tells Santiago was her lover, which likely is not true. Bayardo and the Vicario twins are also clearly guilty—the one for returning the bride, which set vengeance in motion, the others for actually committing the murder. But other less likely characters share guilt in the story as well. Santiago Nasar himself, for instance, sexually abuses his servant, Divina Flor, and in turn Divina—who admits that in the bottom of her heart she wants Santiago dead—likely allows the twins to kill him.

This causal chain of guilt touches less central characters as well—the mayor, for instance, who is too busy worrying about his dominoes game to prevent the murder, and the priest, who is too busy worrying about the bishop's visit. Garcia Marquez suggests that the members of the town—almost all of whom could have stopped the murder—abet it both through their actions and their inactions.

The importance of honor to the culture portrayed in *Chronicle of a Death Foretold* is evident throughout the novel. The murder itself is committed in order to gain back the honor that Angela lost when she had premarital sex, and the honor that was lost to the family with her sex and then failed marriage. Most people in the society tend to think that disputes over honor are better left to those involved; even the jury in the Vicario twins' case find them innocent, because they killed Santiago to win back Angela's honor.

This is another important theme linked to the novel's depiction of Latin American culture. When Angela has premarital sex, and married as a non–virgin, she not only dishonors her family but also fails in her duty to them. According to the society portrayed in *Chronicle of a Death Foretold*, Angela has an obligation to stay a virgin and marry to as high a station as she can (even though she doesn't love the man she marries); if she hadn't had premarital sex, she would have married a very wealthy man. Other characters also have a duty to their family. Among the Vicario's, Pedro goes off to war to earn money for the family, while Pablo stays home to take care of his parents.

The first sentence in chapter five reads "For years we couldn't talk about anything else." Garcia Marquez depicts a society in which everyone in the town knows about the murder that is going to happen except for the man who is going to be murdered—until it's too late. This is one of the central ironies of the book: that everyone is so eager to talk about the murder, but no one is willing to talk about it to the murderer. The natural human tendency to "talk behind someone's back" thus becomes responsible, in part, for a killing.

Also, Garcia Marquez shows us that human memory, as represented by gossip, is fragmented and inconsistent. Like a "big fish" story, the tale of Santiago's death has undergone a gradual transformation in the town's memory up until the time, twenty–seven years after, when the narrator records it. In fact, no one can even agree what the weather was like, let alone the details of the murder.

Human beings live by pattern and routine—that is how we're most comfortable—and the denizens of Santiago's town are no different. Garcia Marquez writes, "Our daily conduct, dominated then by so many linear habits, had suddenly began to spin around a single common anxiety." The murder of Santiago Nasar throws off the whole town and disrupts the peaceful balance of life, thus changing the lives of many people forever. This unusual event, in turn, is patterned into a new way of life for the townspeople, who for years and years after the event discuss it regularly. What had been new becomes routine again.

Another example of the cathartic effect of routine and ritual in human live is the habit of writing to Bayardo that Angela develops. She sends him a letter every week for seventeen years, filled with her deepest feelings. Even though he never reads them, the mere act helps Angela to develop and strengthen as a person. Indeed, her display of tenacity and love is so overwhelming that it eventually convinces Bayardo to come back to her. He doesn't need to know what the letters say; the fact that she has written them so dutifully is enough to convince him of her constancy.

The townsfolk in the novel obsess over Santiago's death "...because none of us could go on living without an exact knowledge of the place and mission assigned to us by fate." The narrator of the novel spends much of his ink in convincing us, or convincing himself, that Santiago Nasar was fated to die under the knives of the Vicario brothers at the specific time and place that the event happens. He fills his narrative with forebodings and omens, all of which clearly point to his death before it happens, though no one is able to interpret them and deter the act.

However, the book also invites consideration that the role of fate is not so strong as the townspeople come to believe. They all share a part in Santiago's murder—whether because they endorse the sense of "honor" that insisted upon a death or because they actually neglected to warn Santiago of the danger he was in. So the emphasis on fate, in this light, acts as a collective alleviation of guilt. The townsfolk desperately want to believe that the death was truly "foretold," that it couldn't have been stopped, thus disburdening them of the moral weight of having killed an innocent member of their society.

Machismo—an important part of *Chronicle of a Death Foretold*—can be seen in the emphasis on male pride in the novel and on the sexual behavior of the male characters. The men take pride in visiting Maria Cervantes's brothel, where they use women for sex. They are not ashamed of their actions, because their society endorses such desires and deeds. When Bayardo San Roman returns Angela Vicario, he demonstrates machismo—a woman is only worth marrying, he suggests, when she is a virgin; after that she is soiled. The Vicario brothers' murder of Santiago Nasar is also a machismo act—an attempt to take back Angela's honor by killing the man who deflowered her. As the string of events in the novel shows, the severe emphasis on masculine and feminine behavior leads to injustice. One man's machismo commits another man's—Bayardo's refusal to accept Angela leads the Vicarios to kill Santiago without trial or evidence.

Major Themes

Glossary of Terms

Blennorhea is the old—fashioned term for gonorrhea, a sexually transmitted disease caused by gonococcal bacteria that affects the mucous membrane chiefly of the genital and urinary tracts and is characterized by an acute purulent discharge and painful or difficult urination, though women often have no symptoms. (dictionary.com)

Short Summary

Chronicle of a Death Foretold describes the murder of a young man, Santiago Nasar, and the events leading to this death. It also follows some of the characters' lives after he is killed.

The murder occurs following Angela Vicario's wedding night, when her wealthy husband, Bayardo San Roman, discovers that she is not a virgin. San Roman returns Angela to her family, where she is brutally interrogated for two hours, finally confessing that Santiago Nasar was the man who deflowered her. Much evidence throughout the story suggests that this accusation is false. However, Angela's brothers, Pedro and Pablo Vicario, take her word for it and kill Santiago in broad daylight in a crowded public square.

Having armed us with this foreknowlege of the murder, Garcia Marquez relates the events leading up to it in non–chronological fashion. He describes the wedding of Angela Vicario and Bayardo San Roman: the grandest celebration the town had ever seen. Bayardo's father was the famous General of the civil wars, General Petronio San Roman, and his family is very wealthy. The formal festivities of the wedding end at 6:00 p.m., when Angela and her groom leave to consummate their marriage; the public stays, however, drinking and dancing until midnight. Some of the wedding guests, including Santiago Nasar, his friend Cristo Bedoya (who narrates the story) and the narrator's brother continue reveling even after midnight, even spending time at Maria Alejandrina Cervantes 's brothel with the Vicario twins, who do not yet know of their sister's disgrace.

Following Angela's confession that Santiago Nasar took her virginity, her twin brothers decide to kill him. They announce their plan to anyone who will listen, in part, it seems, to allow someone to stop them or warn Santiago. Everyone behaves as though someone else will halt the revenge—a local police officer, the mayor, the butcher, and even the local priest all knew of the murder plot—but no one stops it. By six o clock a.m. of the day following the wedding, everyone in town knows the twins are going to kill Santiago. Santiago himself, however, is still unaware. A few try to warn him, including Cristo Bedoya, who has spent the morning with him; Cristo finds out too late, however, and cannot find his friend to warn him.

Eventually, the father of Santiago's fiancee warns him of the plot. He is extremely confused as to why the Vicario twins want to kill him, and his fear leaves him so shaken up that he cannot even find his way back to his house. The Vicario brothers spot him while he stumbles through town. Santiago sprints to his door, which, unfortunately, is locked, due to his mother's belief that he was safe at home and her desire to keep the Vicarios away from him. Pedro and Pablo catch up to Santiago and stab him to death against his own door.

After the murder, an angry group of Arabs, with whom Santiago's father immigrated, chase the Vicarios into a local church. The twins give themselves up and are locked in prison. The Vicario family, meanwhile, ashamed by the whole ordeal, leaves town in disgrace. The twins are tried three years later and acquitted because the murder had been an honor killing. Upon his release, Pablo marries his fiancée, Prudencia Cotes. Pedro reenlists in the army and goes missing in enemy territory.

Meanwhile, the story of Bayardo and Angela unfolds as well. Bayardo San Roman nearly drinks himself to death following the revelation that his bride was not a virgin. He is taken away from the town on a boat by his mother and two sisters. Meanwhile, Angela realizes (while she is being beaten by her mother, in fact) that she loves Bayardo. After coincidentally seeing him in a hotel a few years after their annulled marriage, she begins writing him a letter every week. One day, seventeen years later, Bayardo shows up at her door with one suitcase full of clothes (indicating that he wants to return to her) and one full of her unopened letters.

Summary and Analysis of Chapter 1

Summary

Chronicle of a Death Foretold begins with Santiago Nasar's final morning, clearly stating he is going to be killed. He awakes from uneasy dreams—after which he feels "splattered by bird shit"—to greet a bishop who is supposed to be landing in their town. He mentions the bad dreams to his mother, Placida Linero, who is known to interpret the dreams of others, though even she fails to foresee her son's ensuing death. We are also introduced to the narrator, a good friend of Santiago's, who is telling the story twenty–seven years after the fact.

As he walks to see the bishop, Santiago meets many people who later report that he was in a good mood. He wears unstarched white linen, his suit for special occasions. The narrator states that he was "recovering from the wedding revels [Angela Vicario and Bayardo San Roman had been married the previous evening] in the apostolic lap of Maria Alejandrina Cervantes," the respected local prostitute, on the morning in question. He mentions that Santiago was unarmed, as was his custom, though he owned several guns.

Santiago's mother remembers him on the morning of his death as twenty–one years old, "slim and pale" with "his father's Arab eyelids and curly hair." The Nasar family's two servants, Victoria Guzman and Divina Flor, also see him go to greet the bishop. Victoria had been seduced by Ibrahim Nasar, Santiago's father, years before, and is determined that her daughter not meet the same fate as she; when Santiago makes a pass at Divina, Victoria quietly threatens him with a bloody knife, which startles him. Victoria and Divina both know about the murder plot, though neither mentions it: Victoria because she "thought it was drunkards' talk" and Divina because "in the depths of her heart she wanted them to kill him." As he leaves the house, he grabs Divina's "whole pussy."

Several coincidences immediately arise that make Santiago's death possible: first, he fails to notice a note that had been pushed under the door, warning him in detail of the murder; second, the narrator notes that he generally used the back door of the house, which he failed to do on the day of his death, but which, if he had used it, would have saved his life. On his way to greet the bishop, Santiago passes the milk shop where the twins Pedro and Pablo Vicario are waiting to kill him. However, Clotilde Armenta, the proprietress of the milk shop, convinces them to let Santiago Nasar see the bishop first.

The bishop does not even come ashore, which disappoints many, though Santiago remains in a good mood, reflecting on the magnificent wedding the night before and saying that his own wedding to his fiancée, Flora Miguel, will be just like it. The narrator then turns to Margot; she invites Santiago to breakfast on the day of his murder and he goes home to change first. She then finds out about the plot to kill him—something about how Angela Vicario was returned to her family in shame—and tells her mother, Luisa Santiaga. Luisa, though she has ties to both sides of the conflict, decides to warn Santiago and his mother. On her way to do so, however, someone says, "Don't bother yourself, Luisa Santiaga. They've already killed him."

Analysis

The first paragraph of *Chronicle of a Death Foretold* "foretells" many of the concerns that Garcia Marquez develops throughout the novel. For instance, he focuses on time—mentioning that Santiago woke at 5:30 a.m., that he was killed on a Monday and that the narrator is speaking from twenty–seven years in the future. Specific mentions of time continue throughout the story. Garcia Marquez complements this concern with an unusual structure: instead of unfolding chronologically, the novel is a kind of spiral. Each chapter has its own system of time, tending to circle back on itself. This obsession with time, coupled with Garcia Marquez' unusual structure, suggests the paradox that however journalistically the events of Santiago's death may be recorded, our knowledge can never be certain. Garcia Marquez's descriptions of events almost always include specific times, but they often contradict one another, suggesting that each account "believes" in its own accuracy—though none is wholly accurate.

Also, within the first paragraph, Garcia Marquez introduces the importance of his culture to the ensuing events—especially the role of extrasensory knowledge. Placida Linero is plainly announced to be an "interpreter" of dreams; such occult abilities are treated as commonplace throughout the narrative. Characters consistently respond in an intuitive way to the coming murder. For instance, Santiago's recoil at the sight of the butchered rabbits (a sight that he, a hunter, is well accustomed to and doesn't usually mind) anticipates his own evisceration at the novels end. This tendency to foretell the future also reinforces the treatment of time in the novel: time is not a linear thing, but rather cyclical—hence the spiraling structure of each chapters. Santiago's death is present before it happens and many signs point to it; the characters simply fail to read these signs before it is too late.

Part of this failure stems from the uniqueness of individual perspectives on daily events. Not only does each character fail, in his or her own way, to prevent the murder; the characters in the novel can't even agree upon what the weather was like on the day in question. The inconsistency of memories, thus, is one of the central themes of the work. Throughout, Garcia Marquez replays the same events from different characters' points of views; these differing accounts are clear in themselves, but when compared they reveal, in Garcia Marquez' own words, "a broken mirror of memory [put] back together from so many scattered shards."

This fragmentation of memory corresponds, in turn, to a fragmentation of social responsibility. From the outset, it is apparent that Pedro and Pablo don't really want to kill Santiago—they simply see it as their duty in defending their family honor to attempt the murder. They do all that they can, it seems, to inspire the townsfolk to prevent their success, announcing their intention publicly, even to Santiago's friends. Each member of the society, however, leaves it to the rest to prevent the murder, a collective shirking of conscience that ultimately fails. To some degree, an astonishing number of coincidences occurred to prevent even those who wanted to warn Santiago from doing so; even so, the failure to prevent Santiago's death is a failure of every individual within the society. Even the moral beacons of the town, such as the priest and the mayor, are too self-absorbed to stop a stupid, unjust, easily preventable killing.

Summary and Analysis of Chapter 2

Summary

The second chapter begins with a description of Bayardo San Roman, the groom from the wedding. He is largely a mystery: an extremely wealthy man from a distinguished military family who arrived in town for the first time only sixth months before his wedding. At thirty years old, Bayardo had "the waist of a novice bullfighter, gold eyes, and a skin slowly roasted by saltpeter"; he is accomplished and well liked. Only the narrator's mother, Luisa Santiaga, admits to forebodings about him, but she does so years after the wedding.

Bayardo's ostensible reason for coming to town is simple; he says, "I've been going from town to town looking for someone to marry." When he first sees Angela he calmly realizes that he is going to marry her. He wins her a mother–of–pearl music box at a charity bazaar by buying all of the raffle tickets. She rejects his offer initially, considering him conceited, but Bayardo is a charmer (and much wealthier than the Vicarios) so it doesn't take him long to convince the Vicarios to give him their daughter; they had "scant resources." Pura Vicario, Angela's mother, insists that Bayardo "identify himself properly" before the wedding and so he produces his whole family, makes it known that he is the son of General Petronio San Roman, the "hero of the civil wars of the past century," and presents his beautiful mother and two "provocative" sisters. It doesn't take long for the town to realize that "Bayardo San Roman was going to marry whomever he chose."

Angela, however, remains opposed to marrying him. Her family decides, despite her lack of love for the man, that the marriage will go on, and they arrange a short four–month engagement. Bayardo does all he can to win Angela's love. He asks her what house in the town she likes best and she points out the widower Xius'. Bayardo tells Xius that he wants to buy the house and the widower initially refuses because everything in it had been his wife's; however, when Bayardo Xius makes him an outrageous offer, putting "ten bundles of thousand–peso notes" in front of him, Xius can't refuse any longer. With tears of rage in his eyes, Xius sells Bayardo the house and dies two months later.

One massive problem remains, however: Angela Vicario is not a virgin. She plans to tell her mother and thus cancel the wedding but her friends convince her to fake her virginity by staining her wedding sheets with blood. On the wedding night itself, however, Angela is unable to feign virginity, thus Bayardo returns her to her family.

The narrator next describes the wedding and the feast that followed it. After one problem—Bayardo showed up two hours late and Angela refused to put on her wedding dress until he arrived—the proceedings are magnificent. The narrator, along with his brother Luis Enrique and Cristo Bedoya, were with Santiago Nasar at the wedding and the party the whole night. These four were very close friends; they all cannot believe that if Santiago had taken Angela's virginity, as he is accused, he would not have told him. Bayardo is very friendly with the four during the wedding feast, even discussing the cost of the wedding with Santiago, who is planning a wedding of his own.

The official wedding festivities end at six p.m., when Bayardo and Angela leave to consummate their marriage, but the townsfolk continue celebrating until around midnight, when Santiago Nasar, Cristo Bedoya, Luis Enrique, and the narrator retire to Maria Alejandrina Cervantes's "house of mercies." There they meet the Vicario brothers, who drink and sing with Santiago just five hours before they kill him.

Pura Vicario, Angela's mother, goes to bed around eleven p.m. on the wedding night only to be awakened by three slow knocks on the door. She finds Bayardo San Roman and Angela, in a shredded satin dress and with a towel wrapped around her waist. He leaves Angela with her, saying, "Thank you for everything, Mother. You're a saint." For the next two hours, Pura silently beats Angela—bringing her to the verge of death without even waking her husband. When the twins arrive home, shortly before three, Pedro asks her "who it was." She replies quickly, only taking "the time necessary to say the name," Santiago Nasar.

Analysis

Though Santiago's death is treated as an astonishing and unjust occurrence, Garcia Marquez hands down no simple condemnations in his novel. Every character is flawed and complicated, containing some portion of blame for the sequence of events that culminates in the murder. Chapter Two focuses on one of the most complicated of all these characters: Bayardo. Mysterious, wealthy, reclusive, soft–spoken but with an iron will—Bayardo is difficult to pin down. The narrator says that "he seemed to me like a very sad man," while Luisa Santiaga claims, "He reminded me of the devil" (granted, no one else in the story senses evil in Bayardo). Bayardo is at once capable of ostentatious displays of love and charm and also of ruthless selfishness—as in his transaction with Xius, whom he badgers into selling his home, eventually killing the man.

We also may want to condemn Bayardo for returning Angela, but the way in which he does it, with a soft–spoken thank you to Angela's mother, is strange and unsettling—perhaps engendering a measure of sympathy in the reader. Garcia Marquez does not make Bayardo or Angela simply condemnable any more than he makes Santiago purely loveable (recall Santiago's sexist molesting of Divina Flor, his servant). This is a pattern repeated throughout his novel—and indeed, in many of his other works as well. All of his characters contain obvious imperfections; all share in ultimate guilt but all deserve a measure of the readers' sympathy as well. His purpose, then, is not to blame individuals, but to invite us to consider larger intersections of fate, society, community, and memory.

Which is not to say that the individuals in the novel aren't interesting. Rather, they are full of mystery and strangeness—which Garcia Marquez highlights by using unconventional narrative techniques. For instance, the narrator pointedly mentions that Bayardo San Roman went missing for two hours prior to his wedding, only to arrive "the perfect image of a happy bridegroom." In most novels, we would learn what went on in that two–hour interval, but in this novel we never do. Perhaps there *is* something strange and significant in his absence, perhaps not—Garcia Marquez leaves his novel open to such loose ends, knowing that human life is full of such unexplainable details. His novels—containing both surreal coincidences and their opposite, purely random asides—recreate the perplexity of everyday life: of meaning formation itself.

The chapter closes with Angela's absurdist beating at the hands of her mother—whose rage is so violent that she nearly kills her daughter, yet so controlled that she never makes a sound during the beating. Pura beats her daughter with the same combination of steeliness and propriety that she herself displays—she can't forgive her daughter, it seems, for doing what she would never have done: for surrendering herself.

As for Angela's confession, the narrator makes two things clear: both Santiago's likely innocence and Angela's relative freedom from blame. He writes, when Pedro asks her who did it, that she "only took the time necessary to say the name. She looked for it in the shadows, she found it at first sight among the many, many easily confused names from this world and the other, and she nailed it to the wall with her well–aimed dart, like a butterfly with no will whose sentence has even been written." Santiago's name is picked from the "shadows"—any man's name would have done as well (which implies, perhaps, that all men, as complicit in the patriarchal society that values her only for her virginity, share some blame for what follows). As in so many later events, Santiago is "like a butterfly" pinned to a wall (which, later, he in fact is, by the twins' daggers) by random fate. Angela needs a name in order not to be beaten to death, and the name that comes to her, for whatever reason, is Santiago's.

Summary and Analysis of Chapter 3

Summary

Chapter Three describes the manner in which the Vicario twins went about killing Santiago. It begins with their acquittal, after they had spent three years in prison awaiting trial for the murder, because the homicide was ruled in "legitimate defense of honor."

The narrator then describes the number of people whom the brothers told about their plan to murder Santiago: at least twenty–two. They went about their scheme publicly, even sharpening their knives at the meat market. Next, the brothers visit the milk shop, where they discuss their plan with a policeman, Leandro Pornoy, and with Clotilde. Clotilde is the most concerned of those who are in on the plot, knowing the twins to be scared and immature and thus "capable of everything." She tells her husband, Don Rogelio de la Flor, of the murder plot, only to be dismissed as silly.

Pornoy tells the mayor, Colonel Lazaro Aponte, about the twins plot; he too is dismissive until he discovers that Bayardo San Roman had returned Angela Vicario to her family. Realizing that Santiago Nasar might be in real danger, he takes the twins' knives away and sends them home, failing to detain the brothers (which Clotilde recommends). The mayor then forgets to tell Santiago, only remembering when he sees him waiting to greet the bishop. Clotilde, in an attempt to warn Santiago herself, sends a beggar woman with a message to Victoria Guzman, the Nasars' servant, and also warns Father Amador. Victoria Guzman, however, fails to warn Santiago, and Father Amador is too preoccupied with the bishop's visit to pass on the warning.

Having been sent home, the twins get into a disagreement about whether or not they have fulfilled their duty to try and kill Santiago. Pedro thinks they have but Pablo forces his twin to continue with the plan. With two new knives they head back to the milk shop, meanwhile stopping at the home of Pablo's fiancée, Prudencia Cotes, where they discuss the murder over coffee. Prudencia tells the narrator that she approved of Pablo's design; she later waits three years while he is in prison and marries him upon his release.

Back at the milk shop, Clotilde tries to get the twins drunk on a bottle of rum so that they will be unable to go through with the killing. The twins drink too slowly, though, meanwhile continuing to mention their plan to all who come by.

The narrator then tells how Santiago, the narrator, Luis Enrique, and Cristo Bedoya spent the night in revels while the twins plotted Santiago's death: from Maria Alejandrina Cervantes's whorehouse and they went serenading until after four a.m., including a trip to Xius' old house where they serenaded a lone Bayardo, unaware that he had returned Angela. Santiago Nasar then catches an hour of sleep at his house before the bishop's arrival and the narrator goes to sleep with his lover. Luis Enrique, meanwhile, goes to the milk shop for some cigarettes, where the twins tell him of their plan to kill Santiago. Luis responds by saying "Santiago Nasar is dead" and stumbles home. He does not later remember saying this, and his next memory after passing out is his sister the next morning, crying, "They've killed Santiago Nasar!"

Analysis

This chapter concentrates on the possibility that the Vicario twins didn't really want to kill Santiago Nasar. The narrator writes, "The Vicario brothers…had done much more than could be imagined to have someone to stop them from killing [Santiago], and they had failed." At every step they try merely to enact their vengeance—without ever having to fulfill it. They hang out at the milk shop, more or less waiting to be stopped; then they wait in front of Santiago's door—the last place anyone would have thought he'd go. Thus even the murderers deserve some sympathy. They are acting as mere performers of a public, social expectation to avenge their family honor. The failure of coincidence to inform Santiago of their plot—despite their best efforts to broadcast it—is more to blame, in a way, than they are, for the murder.

However, some individuals clearly carry more of the burden for Santiago's death than others. The mayor, for instance, refuses to detain the twins even when doing so would have been a favor to them. As Clotilde says, he should "spare those poor boys from the horrible duty that's fallen on them." Clotilde, like Cassandra (the Trojan princess in ancient mythology who was gifted with foresight but condemned to be always ignored), is the only character who realizes the danger of the twins' spoken intent. She sees their unwillingness to kill, coupled with their determination to do so if the opportunity comes. And like Cassandra, her warnings go unheeded, lost in the shuffle of others' concerns and a general failure of perspicacity.

But can we truly blame anyone for Santiago's death? Perhaps only abstractions—such as the institution of gender relations presented in the book—are completely blameworthy. Garcia Marquez clearly dramatizes the double standard of sexuality at play in the depicted society: premarital sex is the ultimate transgression against society, while for the men—who hang out at Maria Cervantes' brothel—it is totally acceptable, even for those who are engaged to be married, such as Santiago and the narrator. According to the narrator, Maria Cervantes "did away with my generation's virginity." By "my generation," of course, he means "the men in my generation." His very language contains the double standard that Santiago's death exposes.

And who, after all, is truly "virginal" in the novel? Virginity connotes purity—and Garcia Marquez is careful to show that none of his characters—*not one*—is perfectly pure. All are guilty; each has secrets and weaknesses. Thus he subtly undermines the very notion of valuing "virginity." To value virginity—as a symbol of perfection or unstainedness or what have you—is to misunderstand the human animal, which is full of guilt and corruption and frailty. No wonder, then, that the unrealistic value placed on female virginity leads to unnatural murder—the emphasis is itself unnatural.

Summary and Analysis of Chapter 4

Summary

The chapter begins after Santiago's stabbing, as he is in his death throes on the kitchen floor; his dogs are howling uncontrollably and Placida Linero orders that they be locked up in the stable. At noon they escape and burst back into the house, after which Placida orders them killed. Following the dogs' death the house is silent.

The mayor orders that Santiago's body be refrigerated until Dr. Dionisio Iguaran, who is out of town, can perform an autopsy. Their attempts at refrigeration fail, however; Santiago's body rots until Father Amador, who had briefly attended medical school, is prevailed upon to perform the autopsy. The body comes back badly botched, "as if [they'd] killed him all over again after he was dead," along with the judgment that there were seven fatal stab wounds and many more smaller ones. Father Amador also notes that Santiago's liver revealed a poorly cured case of hepatitis, meaning that he would only have lived a few more years anyway, an opinion later disputed by Dr. Iguaran.

The chapter goes on to describe the fallout after Santiago's death. The narrator, for instance, visits his lover, Maria, only to find her gorging herself: her way of mourning. He falls asleep while mourning with her and is awoken when she tries to make love to him; she soon stops, however, saying, "I can't. You smell of him."

Pedro and Pablo Vicario, who are in jail, also smell Santiago everywhere. They are afraid to sleep, where they commit the murder again in their dreams. Also, they both have horrible excretory problems—Pedro suffers from sergeant's blennorrhea, which makes urination painful, and Pablo suffers from "pestilential diarrhea." They are further troubled because the generally peaceful Arab community had been vengeful after Santiago's death. Eventually Susana Abdala, the ancient matriarch of the Arab immigrants, cures both Pedro's blennorrhea and Pablo's diarrhea.

The narrator relates the fates of the Vicario family: after the debacle, they retire from the town and never return, moving to Manaure instead. The twins insist that their killing was honorable all the way up to their trial day, when they are absolved. They move to Riohacha near Manaure where Pablo marries Prudencia and becomes a goldsmith. Pedro, meanwhile, reenlists in the army and disappears one morning in enemy territory.

Bayardo's fate is also related: Colonel Aponte finds him in Xius' house, still wearing his wedding clothes, "in the last stages of ethylic intoxication." His mother and two sisters come and carry him to their boat in a hammock, still drunk and looking as though he was dead.

Angela and her mother, meanwhile, move to an Indian village in the upper Guajira. The narrator notes that he saw her there twenty–three years after the murder and is surprised by "the way in which she'd ended up understanding her own life." She has matured and grown witty and she doesn't shy away from recounting the details of the wedding and murder, though she never tells the identity of her true lover.

Angela tells the narrator the while her mother was beating her she realized that she loved Bayardo. One day long afterwards she saw him in a hotel lobby in Riohacha and from that day on she "went crazy over him." She wrote him letters continually though he never replied, and in so doing "she became lucid, overbearing, mistress of her own free will, and she became a virgin again just for him, and she recognized no other authority than her own nor any other service than that of her obsession." She wrote him a letter once a week for seventeen years and finally Bayardo arrived at her house, old fat and balding, with two suitcases, one filled with clothing "in order to stay," and another with almost two thousand letters that she'd written to him, all unopened.

Analysis

Santiago Nasar's dogs, first shown in Chapter One begging for the rabbits' innards while Victoria Guzman cooks, make a memorable repeat appearance. Divina Flor, while holding the dogs off in Chapter Four, screams, "Help me! What they want is to eat his guts." Thus, once again, time has looped back on itself: Santiago's death, present from the beginning, has come to pass: the eviscerated white rabbit has become the eviscerated youth in white linens. Such repetitions emphasize the death's "foretold" nature; no one, Garcia Marquez, could have prevented this innocent from dying.

And it's not just the dogs that are obsessed with guts in the fourth chapter. Another main event of the section is Father Amador's botched autopsy of Santiago, whose gore and wounds evoke much of the meaning of this passage. For a good deal of the book, Santiago is treated as a sort of idea, a man maligned by fate and misremembered by the community that failed him. In Chapter Four, however, Garcia Marquez shows him as a human being. His death throes are described in horrific, close detail, and Garcia Marquez makes much of the comparison to Jesus Christ, noting stigmata in Santiago's left hand. Like Christ, Santiago has been sacrificed for a sin that he (likely) did not commit; he is a scapegoat, a sacrificial lamb in white linen. And like Christ, his martyrdom is recorded in gruesome physical detail.

And the autopsy—a second death, as his mother notes—is just as disrespectful and senseless as the murder itself. It tells us nothing new at all. Perhaps its only function is to make the villagers feel better about their failure to prevent the death—after all, Father Amador "discovers" that Santiago would only have lived a short while longer anyway due to an enlarged liver. We can doubt very much the truth of this conclusion; it seems merely to serve as a sort of umbrage for a guilty town. As with the constant talk of coincidences, the town would rather blame fate for Santiago's death than scrutinize themselves.

Similarly, the majority of townsfolk don't even consider Santiago a victim of this murder. They consider Bayardo the only victim, because only he has lost honor, assuming that Santiago slept with Angela and thus deserved his death and that Angela, through Santiago's killing, has been redeemed. Again, as with the autopsy, this is umbrage from collective guilt: we know how unlikely it is that Santiago slept with Angela, but the townsfolk by and large seem to require a simple explanation for his death. They need him to be guilty—though he probably isn't—so that they don't have to see themselves as guilty. Garcia Marquez, however, insinuates that everyone in the town shares the stain of guilt.

And every character shares innocence as well. Even Angela, who seems easiest to condemn for her randomly chosen death sentence, finds redemption. She explains to the narrator many years after that the reason she could not fake her virginity—in other words, fake her virtue—is that she was, in fact virtuous. He writes that she had a "pure decency...carried hidden inside the solidity her mother had imposed." Her willingness to reveal her indecency (her lost virginity) is, in fact, an act of decency; Angela, like everyone, contains both innocence and corruption. She is corrupt in the weak bodily sense that her patriarchal society values—she is deflowered. But within herself she is pure, uncorrupt. As she says, she is a second virgin. Then again, she condemns an innocent man and stands by her lie forever. We will never get a simple reading on a Garcia Marquez character; they are both deceived and deceivers, innocents and fallen, human through and through.

Finally, one of the most magical parts of this novel is the return of Bayardo with his suitcase full of unopened letters. The gesture captures the incredible sense of grief and love that follows a betrayal: Bayardo can't bring himself to read the letters, Angela can't bring herself to stop writing them. When he returns, toting seventeen years of Angela's most anguished outpourings, it is as though he brings her life back with him. The same solid pure decency that kept her from deceiving Bayardo ultimately wins him back; her stubborn reliance on her self–defined—not society–defined—virtue. Angela is a charming, witty woman, as full of mystery as her lover when the novel closes, making it all the easier to forgive her youthful, extorted condemnation of Santiago.

Summary and Analysis of Chapter 5

Summary

For years after, no one in town can discuss anything but the murder. They become obsessed with the number of coincidences that aligned in order to make the murder possible; some are never able to forgive themselves for their part in the murder. For instance, while Placida is able to explain why she locked the main door (Divina swore she'd seen Santiago enter and go upstairs), she can't forgive herself for failing to notice the omens in Santiago's dreams.

The narrator shifts to twelve days after the murder, when the investigating magistrate comes to town. The magistrate, who is unnamed, notes in the margins of the case that "he never thought it legitimate that life should make use of so many coincidences forbidden literature." He is further alarmed at "not having found a single clue, not even the most improbable, that Santiago Nasar had been the cause of the wrong."

Shifting to the murder day, we learn that the twins tell Santiago's good friend Indalecio Pardo, about their plan. Indalecio loses the nerve to warn Santiago when he sees him. On the morning, Santiago walks with Cristo Bedoya, who notices strange looks among the crowd but is not yet aware of the plan. The crowd parts for them, not wanting to touch a man who will soon die.

After Cristo and Santiago part, Yamil Shaium, an Arab who had immigrated with Santiago Nasar's father, warns Cristo of the plot, but Cristo is unable to find Santiago again. Somehow, no one has seen him enter his fiancée's home off the square. Cristo goes to Santiago's house, where he tells Victoria of the plot (she already knows); when he cannot find Santiago he leaves without telling Placida, for want of frightening her.

Back in the square, Pedro Vicario calls to Cristo to warn Santiago but Cristo is still unable to find his friend. He tells Colonel Aponte, who swears that he sent the twins home but agrees to take care of the matter again. Instead the mayor stops by the social club to check on a dominoes date. Cristo meanwhile goes to the narrator's house, where he assumes Santiago must have gone, only to hear distant shouting and learn that he was too late.

When Santiago arrives at her house, his fiancée Flora, who knew of the plot, furiously returns his love letters to her, saying, "Here you are, and I hope they kill you!" She later explains that she didn't believe they would really kill Santiago but thought they would force him to marry Angela. Santiago has no idea what caused her outburst and calls after her, rousing the whole family, at which point Flora's father, Nahir Miguel, informs him of the plot. Santiago is totally confused, and thus clearly innocent, so Nahir tells him to hide in their house or take a rifle for protection.

Santiago, however, leaves without the rifle, afraid and baffled—unable even to find his own house. The twins see him and walk after him; Clotilde Armenta screams for Santiago to run. Meanwhile, Victoria had finally told Placida about the murder plot; Placida asks Divina if her son is at home, and when Divina swears that he is, she locks the door, seeing the Vicario brothers running at the house with their knives out. Santiago, shut out of his own house seconds too late, is killed. The twins stab him repeatedly, including a horizontal slash across his stomach that releases his viscera.

Just then, a group of angry Arab immigrants brandishing guns chase the twins to the church. Santiago stumbles into the house through the back door "that had been open since six" and dies in the kitchen.

Analysis

This chapter does not contain much that is new—we've already seen these events before, several times. It serves rather to place these events in a larger, literary context, mostly through the testimony of the visiting judge. This investigating magistrate—who interprets the events of this novel much like a reader or a critic himself—clearly sides with many of the conclusions that Garcia Marquez has already invited us to accept. He concludes that Santiago Nasar's behavior during the morning of his death was "overwhelming proof of his innocence" and that Angela's impassivity in naming him as her perpetrator suggested the she was lying. Moreover, the judge determines that the Vicario brothers don't want to murder Santiago—they even tell Indalecio Pardo, a good friend of Santiago Nasar's, about their plan to kill him; when Clotilde Armenta tells him to warn Santiago, Pedro tells him, "Don't bother. No matter what, he's as good as dead already." This statement was "too obvious a challenge;" the twins "must have thought that he was just the right person to stop the crime without bringing any shame on them."

But the magistrate's purpose is not just to tie up these loose ends. After all, we could be reasonably sure that Santiago is innocent and that the Vicarios are ambivalent about killing him well before the magistrate passes his judgment. What the magistrate brings that is new is a sense of the preceding events as literature. The judge in this chapter states that "he never thought it legitimate that life should make use of so many coincidences forbidden literature." This is a tongue–in–cheek comment if ever there was one, as the proceeding—though based on a real event—is, in fact literature. Indeed, Garcia Marquez' novel is literature, to a great degree, *because of*, not *in spite of*, the use of coincidences.

Garcia Marquez uses these coincidences in two ways, both of which get at the deepest resonances of the novel. On the one hand, the series of unbelievable chances that result in Santiago's death suggest that the death was fated, that no one could have stopped it. There is a sense of magic in this reading, of inescapable destiny. This theme has been developed from the very first words of the book, even from the book's very title. Santiago's death is "foretold." He dreams ominous dreams, responds strangely to the rabbit guts, etc. All the way until his death, it is as though fate works through the townsfolk, keeping them from warning him until it's too late. Even Santiago himself is, in this reading, complicit in his own death. He goes for the front door, resulting in his murder—not the back, which would have saved him. As characters comment throughout the book, he's already dead. There's no saving him.

But on the other hand, maybe all of these coincidences aren't coincidences at all. The narrator records them twenty–seven years after the fact, remember, and the people he interviews seem uniformly willing to shirk their complicity in the murder onto a sense of the murder's fatedness. Taking the two prongs of "magical realism": if the sense of fate in the book is what makes it magical, it is this attentiveness to magic as a human psychological condition that makes the book realistic. Only in hindsight do these coincidences seem so bafflingly coincidental. Perhaps, in reality, they are simply instances of selfishness and strategy—Divina Flora, remember, has reason to hate Santiago, and she may very well cause his death when she tells Santiago's mother that her son is safe upstairs—with a reasonable measure of chance. Perhaps the very act of calling Santiago's death a "series of coincidences" is merely a collective purging of conscience. He could have been saved—he *should* have been saved—but he wasn't, and so, in hindsight, people pretend he never could have been saved, or that he deserved to die, or that he would have died anyway of an "enlarged liver."

Given that Garcia Marquez based this novel on the real–life death of a friend of his, it seems reasonably that the second reading might be the more accurate. His story is not just a beautiful evocation of magic and fate, it is a specific condemnation of cultural practices—such as honor killings and enforced virginity—that result in chaotic, vigilante "justice." Santiago's death, though beautifully and carefully crafted in the language of destiny, is not destined. It is the result of moral failure, for which all members of society—including Santiago himself—can assume some burden of the guilt.

Suggested Essay Questions

1. Discuss the structure of the novel. How is it laid out—linearly, cyclically, randomly, or in some other way? How does this structure inform the novel's themes?

2. Who are what is most to blame for Santiago Nasar's murder and why? Is any person or social institution more to blame for Santiago's murder than others?

3. The narrator states that most of the townspeople thought that the main victim of the tragedy was Bayardo San Roman. Do you agree with their conclusion? Why or why not?

4. How important is the setting of the novel (in a small Colombian town)? In what ways does Colombian culture find expression in the people and events of the novel?

5. Discuss gender relations in the novel. How are men and women treated differently? Does this different treatment affect the novel's development? What do you believe to be Garcia Marquez' position with regard to this different treatment of men and women?

6. Look for evidence as to whether or not Santiago was really Angela's lover. Argue for or against this possibility.

7. Why do you think that Angela chose Santiago Nasar as her scapegoat? Would the novel have been different if she had chosen another character? What does it mean for Angela to have chosen a scapegoat at all?

8. What role do coincidences play in the novel? What do these coincidences mean in terms of the narrative? Is fate solely—or at least largely—responsible for Santiago's death? How does narrative itself generally treat coincidences? Pay close attention to the judges remark that many of the coincidences in the event are not "allowed" to literature.

9. Garcia Marquez is a famous proponent of magical realism. Citing specific examples, discuss the existence or non–existence of this genre in *Chronicle of a Death Foretold*

10. Discuss animal imagery in *Chronicle of a Death Foretold*, concentrating on Santiago in particular. Note his dream of birds, the butterfly analogy in the discussion of Angela's accusation, and other instances in which Santiago is compared, expressly or obliquely, to an animal. Along these lines, what part do Santiago Nasar's dogs play in the novel?

The Boom: Latin American Literature in the mid to late 1900s

The "boom period" in Latin American Literature usually refers to the span from the 1950s to the 1970s in which Latin American Literature attained publicity that it had not known before. Important authors in the "boom" included Julio Cortazar, Manuel Puig, Carlos Fuentes, Mario Vargas Llosa, Jose Donoso, and Gabriel Garcia Marquez. These Latin American authors were greatly influenced by European and American authors of the generations preceding them, especially those who experimented with novelistic structure and chronology. Such authors include William Faulkner, James Joyce, Henry James and Virginia Woolf. The "boom" brought about a new genre of writing coined "magic realism" or "magical realism," because these Latin American novels tended to blend magic and dream–like features with an attentiveness to everyday reality.

Garcia Marquez's *One Hundred Years of Solitude* is often considered one of the most prominent works of the "boom" period. While *Chronicle of a Death Foretold* was published in 1981, which many consider to be after the "boom" period had ended, it clearly includes many of the aspects of that literary time. For instance, not only does *Chronicle of a Death Foretold* incorporate features of magic realism constantly through novel—including characters who practice the occult as well as several evil omens—but also Garcia Marquez experiments with structure and the fragmentation of time, two main characteristics of a "boom" novel.

Garcia Marquez was also ahead of his time when he wrote *Chronicle of a Death Foretold* in that he anticipated the recent Latin American trend of writing about the working classes. Authors of the recent "post–boom" period often incorporate young lower class characters in their novels. Marquez deals with the class struggles in Columbia, using Santiago Nasar to represent the upper middle–class, and characters such as Angela Vicario and her brothers to represent the lower working–class. *Chronicle of a Death Foretold* was written before the themes of class struggle became popular in Latin American novels, and is therefore a harbinger of the most recent Latin American literature.

Author of ClassicNote and Sources

Hannah Wallace, author of ClassicNote. Completed on September 02, 2006, copyright held by GradeSaver.

Updated and revised W.C. Miller September 20, 2006. Copyright held by GradeSaver.

Gabriel Garcia Marquez. Chronicle of a Death Foretold. New York: Vintage Books, 2003.

Ruben Pelayo. Gabriel Garcia Marquez: A Critical Companion. Westport, CT: Greenwood Press, 2001.

Editor: Harold Bloom. Gabriel Garcia Marquez. New York: Chelsea House Publishers, 1999.

Jacqueline Parker. "Chronicle of a Death Foretold by Gabriel Garcia Marquez." 2006-08-25.
<http://www.randomhouse.com/acmart/catalog/display.pperl?isbn=9781400034710.

Editor-in-Charge Tore Frängsmyr, Editor Sture Allén. "Gabriel Garcia Marquez: The Nobel Prize in Literature 1982." 2006-08-29.
<http://nobelprize.org/nobel_prizes/literature/laureates/1982/marquez-bio.html>.

"Garcia Marquez." 2006-08-24.
<http://www.themodernword.com/gabo/gabo_biography.html>.

"Dictionary.com." 2006-09-02.
<http://dictionary.reference.com/search?q=gonorrhea.

Essay: Honor Codes and Ritual Contrition

by Anonymous
April 23, 2003

Gabriel Garcia Marquez's Chronicle of a Death Foretold is a relatively small book, yet it is open to countless interpretations as to the book's overall purpose. Here I will discuss two such interpretations: Isabel Alvarez–Borland's analysis sees the novella as asking why a senseless murder was allowed to occur; Carlos J. Alonso focuses on the point of the text being a ritual means for redemption. Both analyses are strongly argued and very conceivable, offering valuable insights into the text and developing meaningful interpretations.

Isabel Alvarez–Borland's "From Mystery to Parody: (Re)Readings of Garcia Marquez's Cronica de una muerte anunciada" asks why the town allowed the murder to transpire when there was ample opportunity to stop it. The analysis blames the town's hypocritical honor codes for Santiago Nasar's death and indicts the townspeople for their complicity. In this society, the women must remain virgins until marriage or else they are considered defiled and damaged. The men, on the other hand, seem to do as they please with no social repercussions. They even solicit whores before and even after marriage. For example, the narrator declares of Maria Alejandrina Cervantes, the town whore, "It was she who did away with my generation's virginity" (Garcia Marquez 74).

Indeed, in this view, the townspeople's mentality is to blame. This social code is a blatant double standard, strictly censoring the women's sexuality while the men go out and have promiscuous sex. In reality, Santiago is himself quite the womanizer, going around "nipping the bud of any wayward virgin who began showing up in those woods" (104). The town is so entrenched in these antiquated beliefs that the Vicario brothers are eventually absolved of the murder. The court accepts the argument that the murder was a necessary defense of honor, and after three years in prison, they are free men.

The murder plot is known to almost everyone because the Vicario brothers make no secret of their plan. The town's knowledge of the murder plot is illustrated by the narrator's ironic comment, "There had never been a death more foretold" (57). The death is foretold to practically everyone except for Santiago himself. It seems absurd to think that the murder is allowed to take place, or that Santiago is not warned sooner, with such an abundance of foreknowledge.

Pablo and Pedro Vicario feel so strongly bound by their society's honor codes that they kill a man. In fact, the reader gets the sense that the Vicario brothers do not even want to kill Santiago; they are just doing it because they feel duty bound to do so. They believe that their family's honor can only be redeemed through the public murder of Santiago. They cannot back down because the honor code binds them to a course of action. The amount of social pressure that is upon the boys can be seen in Prudencia Cotes's startling statement, "I knew what they were up to...and I didn't only agree, I never would have married [Pablo] if he hadn't done what a man should do" (72). The only way they can be stopped is by the people around them, but the townspeople fail to prevent the murder. The town accepts and lives by this honor code which allows murder to regain respect. By failing to stop the murder, every person has, to some extent, been an accomplice to the crime.

Alvarez–Borland's analysis goes on to state that the last two sections of the story can be viewed as the author's condemnation of the townspeople. In the second to last section, the narrator describes the autopsy as a massacre, a murder after the murder. This coupled with the grisly depiction of the actual murder "can thus be viewed as a motivation for the reader to realize, with the implied author, the dire consequences of hypocritical honor codes" (Alvarez–Borland 221). Also, as the analysis points out, the point of view changes from "I" to "we" in the fifth section, which "can be taken as further evidence of the condemnation by the author of the narrator and the townspeople, thus presenting a scathing comment on the corruption of their moral values as well as their institutions" (221). The book reveals the town as it really is: ugly and dirty.

In fact, after the crime that these antiquated honor codes have led to takes place, the entire town seems to fall apart. Filled with a collective guilt, the town is changed forever, perhaps symbolized by Bayardo San Roman's house and car: "The house began to crumble. The wedding car was falling apart by the door, and finally nothing remained except its weather–rotted carcass" (Garcia Marquez 100). Don Rogelio de la Flore dies at the shock of seeing how Santiago is murdered. Santiago's former fiance, Flora Miguel, runs away with a lieutenant who then prostitutes her in a nearby town. Divina Flore, now overweight and faded, sits surrounded by her children from various fathers. Every person suffers a different fate, from death to insanity to that of the narrator, but it seems certain that the town has paid the price for their sins.

While Alvarez–Borland's analysis looks at Chronicle of a Death Foretold as a text that explores why the murder is allowed to happen, Carlos J. Alonso argues that the novella's purpose is to reenact the murder as an attempt at redemption. In "Writing and Ritual in Chronicle of a Death Foretold" he asserts that the text is merely a means of recreating the crime, not understanding or accounting for it. The ritual reenactment of the offense "is an attempt to endow the crime with the prescribed order of ceremony, thereby overcoming the centrifugal and fortuitous character of the original events" (Alonso 265). The townspeople feel a tension that they try to alleviate by calling the day's events fate. They find themselves constantly "trying to give order to the chain of many chance events that [have] made absurdity possible, and it [is] obvious that [they aren't] doing it from an urge to clear up mysteries but because none of [them can] go on living without an exact knowledge of the place and the mission assigned to [them] by fate" (Garcia Marquez 113). Calling it fate makes

Essay: Honor Codes and Ritual Contrition

it easier to accept that a murder that could have and should have been prevented took place. It serves to lessen the guilt felt by the townspeople.

The story, Alonso argues, is told simply for the cathartic nature of storytelling. The chronicle's purpose is the reliving of the murder in an attempt to relieve the town's and the narrator's tension and guilt. However, the very fact that the story is a ritual reenactment means that it can never serve as the instrument of redemption. With each reading and rereading of the story, the reader relives the murder. It is an endless cycle of violence that is never cleansed. In fact, Santiago is killed many times throughout the text. There is, of course, the grisly murder that appears at the end of the book, but Santiago Nasar also dies symbolically in his dreams. The night before his murder, for instance, Santiago's dream contains the unlucky omen of birds. His mother, who is an experienced interpreter of dreams, curiously misreads her son's warning, something she will never forgive herself for. Victoria Guzman also kills Santiago symbolically in the kitchen as she guts the rabbits, to Santiago's disgust, thereby foreshadowing his own disembowelment. Also, as mentioned above, the autopsy is a gruesome mess in which Santiago is butchered once more. With the continual act of murder after murder, the book can offer no contrition.

The only information that is gained from reading the story is the same limited data that is available to the narrator. He does not uncover any more truly significant facts than the investigating magistrate before him. He does not discover the truth about Santiago Nasar's guilt or innocence. It is clear that the reader must look beyond this for the true purpose of the story. It may be a condemnation of medieval traditions and beliefs, or it may be a pass at penitence. Perhaps it is a comment on the corollaries of murder or a dissertation on the psychology of mass complicity. The text is open to several different interpretations, and thus should be approached with an open mind.

Works Cited

Alonso, Carlso J. "Writing and Ritual in Chronicle of a Death Foretold." Modern Critical Views: Gabriel Garcia Marquez. Ed. Harold Bloom. New York: Chelsea House, 1989. 257–269.

Alvarez–Borland, Isabel. "From Mystery to Parody: (Re)Readings of Garcia Marquez's Cronica de una muerte anunciada." Modern Critical Views: Gabriel Garcia Marquez. Ed. Harold Bloom. New York: Chelsea House, 1989. 219–226.

Garcia Marquez, Gabriel. Chronicle of a Death Foretold. New York: Ballantine, 1982.

Quiz 1

1. **What time did Santiago get up to see the bishop?**
   A. 5:00 am
   B. 6:00 am
   C. 5:30 am
   D. 5:45 am

2. **What day was Santiago Nasar murdered?**
   A. Monday
   B. Tuesday
   C. Thursday
   D. Wednesday

3. **When was Placida Linero a good interpreter of dreams?**
   A. before eating
   B. before drinking
   C. before noon
   D. before brushing her teeth

4. **What bad omen was in Santiago Nasar's dreams in the days before his murder?**
   A. Fireflies
   B. Dogs
   C. Birds
   D. Trees

5. **Who was the narrator with at the time of the murder?**
   A. Margot
   B. Cristo Bedoya
   C. Maria Alejandrina Cervantes
   D. Luis Enrique

6. **What color was Santiago's outfit when he was killed?**
   A. Tan
   B. Blue
   C. White
   D. Brown

7. **Where did Santiago keep his gun while he was sleeping?**
   A. In the dresser drawer
   B. On his bed table
   C. What gun?
   D. In his pillowcase

8. **Did Santiago keep his guns loaded?**
   A. No
   B. n/a
   C. n/a
   D. Yes

9. **How old was Santiago Nasar?**
   A. 20
   B. 21
   C. 22
   D. 23

10. **Who was Santiago's fiancee?**
    A. Margot
    B. Prudencia Cotes
    C. Purisma del Carmen
    D. Flora Miguel

11. **Who was Victoria Guzman seduced by?**
    A. Ibrahim Nasar
    B. Cristo Bedoya
    C. Santiago Nasar
    D. Yamil Shaium

12. **Was Divina Flor the daughter of #11?**
    A. N/A
    B. Unknown
    C. No
    D. Yes

13. **What does Victoria Guzman feed the dogs?**
    A. Rabbit innards
    B. Partridge legs
    C. Leftover steak
    D. Rabbit feet

14. **Which door did Santiago almost always take to go outside?**
    A. He never left the house. ever.
    B. Main/Front Door
    C. Back Door
    D. Side Door

15. **Which door did Santiago take on the day he was murdered?**
    A. Window
    B. Main/Front Door
    C. Back Door
    D. Side Door

16. **What was the only thing that Ibrahim Nasar left intact in the parlor?**
    A. an expensive painting
    B. a door to the attic
    C. an old table
    D. a spiral staircase

17. **What name did the door to the square aquire after the murder?**
    A. Coincidental Murderer
    B. Stabbed Door
    C. Door of Death
    D. The Fatal Door

18. **What made the loud uproar as Santiago left his house?**
    A. People
    B. Roosters
    C. Dogs
    D. Cows

19. How old were Pedro and Pablo Vicario?
    A. 22
    B. 23
    C. 24
    D. 25

20. What were the twins wearing when they killed Santiago?
    A. their wedding suits
    B. pajamas
    C. blue jeans
    D. an outfit of white linen

21. What did the twins wrap their knives in?
    A. Nothing
    B. Wrapping paper
    C. Newspaper
    D. Cloth

22. Who convinces the twins to wait until after the bishop's visit to kill Santiago?
    A. Margot
    B. Cristo Bedoya
    C. Clotilde Armenta
    D. Yamil Shaium

23. Did the bishop get off the boat?
    A. N/A
    B. No
    C. N/A
    D. Yes

24. What did Purisma del Carmen usually go by?
    A. Pura del Carmen
    B. Puri del Carmen
    C. Pura Vicario
    D. Puri Vicario

25. **Who was Santiago Nasar's godmother?**
   A. the narrator's mother
   B. the narrator's sister (the nun)
   C. Clotilde Armenta
   D. Purisma del Carmen

Quiz 1 Answer Key

1. **(C)** 5:30 am
2. **(A)** Monday
3. **(A)** before eating
4. **(C)** Birds
5. **(C)** Maria Alejandrina Cervantes
6. **(C)** White
7. **(D)** In his pillowcase
8. **(A)** No
9. **(B)** 21
10. **(D)** Flora Miguel
11. **(A)** Ibrahim Nasar
12. **(C)** No
13. **(A)** Rabbit innards
14. **(C)** Back Door
15. **(B)** Main/Front Door
16. **(D)** a spiral staircase
17. **(D)** The Fatal Door
18. **(B)** Roosters
19. **(C)** 24
20. **(A)** their wedding suits
21. **(C)** Newspaper
22. **(C)** Clotilde Armenta
23. **(B)** No
24. **(C)** Pura Vicario
25. **(A)** the narrator's mother

Quiz 2

1. What month did Bayardo San Roman come to the town?
   A. August
   B. October
   C. June
   D. July

2. What color were Bayardo's eyes?
   A. Golden
   B. Turquoise
   C. Green
   D. Brown

3. When did Bayardo first see Angela Vicario?
   A. At the Charity Bazaar, as she was "singing out the raffle numbers"
   B. When she crossed the square outside his boarding house
   C. When they ran into each other in the square
   D. As he was getting off his boat at the docks

4. What did Bayardo win Angela at the charity bazaar?
   A. Turquoise earrings
   B. A gold necklace
   C. A dog
   D. A mother-of-pearl music box

5. What did Santiago Nasar call Angela Vicario (to the narrator)?
   A. Fool
   B. Dolt
   C. Twit
   D. Ninny

6. How many sisters does Bayardo San Roman have?
   A. One
   B. Two
   C. None
   D. Three

7. What brand of car do Bayardo's parents drive?
   A. Toyota
   B. Cadillac
   C. Ford
   D. Lexus

8. Who is sitting at the dominoes table with Bayardo and Xius?
   A. Cristo Bedoya
   B. Dr. Dionisio Iguaran
   C. Yamil Shaium
   D. Luis Enrique

9. How much does Bayardo claim that the whole wedding cost?
   A. 9,000 Pesos
   B. 20,000 Pesos
   C. 18,000 Pesos
   D. 28,000 Pesos

10. Who did the narrator propose to at the wedding festivities?
    A. Margot
    B. Maria Alejandrina Cervantes
    C. Mercedes Barcha
    D. Flora Miguel

11. How old was the woman in #10?
    A. just out of primary school
    B. early 20s
    C. early 40s
    D. just out of college

12. What time did the formal wedding festivities end?
    A. 6:00 pm
    B. 7:00 pm
    C. 8:00 pm
    D. 9:00 pm

13. **What time did the "public spree" finish up?**
    A. Midnight
    B. 1 am
    C. 11 pm
    D. 1:20 am

14. **Which twin asked Angela who her lover was?**
    A. Pablo Vicario
    B. Pedro Vicario
    C. It wasn't a twin, it was her father.
    D. It wasn't a twin, it was her mother.

15. **What did the twins' lawyer claim in their defense?**
    A. Not guilty because of self defense
    B. Not guilty because of mental defect
    C. Homicide in legitimate defense of honor
    D. Innocent of committing the crime

16. **Who lead the group of Arabs that chased the twins to the church?**
    A. Cristo Bedoya
    B. Placida Linero
    C. Yamil Shaium
    D. Susana Abdala

17. **Where did the twins wait for Santiago Nasar?**
    A. Clotilde Armenta's milk shop
    B. At Santiago's back door
    C. The boat dock
    D. Flora Miguel's house

18. **Who warned the police officer of the murder plot?**
    A. Margot
    B. Cristo Bedoya
    C. Faustino Santos
    D. Luis Enrique

19. **What was the police officer's name?**
    A. Lazaro Aponte
    B. Leandro Pornoy
    C. Indalecio Pardo
    D. Nahir Miguel

20. **Who told the mayor that Angela had been returned to her family by Bayardo?**
    A. Cristo Bedoya
    B. His wife
    C. Police officer
    D. the Narrator

21. **What disease did Pedro Vicario return from the army with?**
    A. Herpes
    B. Chlamydia
    C. Hepatitis
    D. Blennorrhea

22. **Who is Pablo Vicario's fiancee?**
    A. Margot
    B. Maria Alejandrina Cervantes
    C. Prudencia Cotes
    D. Flora Miguel

23. **Who, according to the narrator, "did away with [his] generation's virginity"?**
    A. Angela Vicario
    B. Maria Alejandrina Cervantes
    C. Purisma del Carmen
    D. Flora Miguel

24. **Who first told Victoria Guzman about the murder plot?**
    A. Cristo Bedoya
    B. Placida Linero
    C. Clotilde Armenta
    D. Beggar woman

25. **Did Father Amador receive Clotilde's warning about the murder plot?**
    A. N/A
    B. No
    C. Yes, but it was too late to do anything.
    D. Yes

Quiz 2 Answer Key

1. **(A)** August
2. **(A)** Golden
3. **(B)** When she crossed the square outside his boarding house
4. **(D)** A mother–of–pearl music box
5. **(D)** Ninny
6. **(B)** Two
7. **(C)** Ford
8. **(B)** Dr. Dionisio Iguaran
9. **(C)** 18,000 Pesos
10. **(C)** Mercedes Barcha
11. **(A)** just out of primary school
12. **(A)** 6:00 pm
13. **(A)** Midnight
14. **(B)** Pedro Vicario
15. **(C)** Homicide in legitimate defense of honor
16. **(C)** Yamil Shaium
17. **(A)** Clotilde Armenta's milk shop
18. **(C)** Faustino Santos
19. **(B)** Leandro Pornoy
20. **(B)** His wife
21. **(D)** Blennorrhea
22. **(C)** Prudencia Cotes
23. **(B)** Maria Alejandrina Cervantes
24. **(D)** Beggar woman
25. **(D)** Yes

Quiz 3

1. **Who did the autopsy on Santiago Nasar's body?**
   A. Cristo Bedoya
   B. Dr. Dionisio Iguaran
   C. Luis Enrique
   D. Father Amador

2. **Who should have done the autopsy?**
   A. Cristo Bedoya
   B. Dr. Dionisio Iguaran
   C. Luis Enrique
   D. Father Amador

3. **What did the dogs want to do to Santiago's body?**
   A. "smell it"
   B. "lick his wounds"
   C. "eat his guts"
   D. "play with it"

4. **Who gave the order to kill the dogs?**
   A. Cristo Bedoya
   B. Placida Linero
   C. Divina Flor
   D. Luis Enrique

5. **What was found in Santiago's stomach during the autopsy?**
   A. a dog tag
   B. a gold necklace
   C. a pen
   D. a gold medal

6. **What wound was Christ–like?**
   A. A stigma on his left hand
   B. A stigma on his left foot
   C. A stigma on his right hand
   D. A stigma on his right foot

7. **What did Father Amador claim that Santiago would have died from in a few years?**
    A. Bacterial Meningitis
    B. Hepatitis
    C. Schreibeis
    D. Blennorrhea

8. **How did Maria Cervantes cope with grief?**
    A. Crying
    B. Picking fights
    C. Eating disproportionate amounts of food
    D. Sex

9. **Why couldn't Maria Cervantes sleep with the narrator after Santiago's death?**
    A. the narrator looked like Santiago
    B. the narrator wasn't up for it
    C. the narrator was friends with Santiago
    D. the narrator smelled of Santiago

10. **What problem did Pablo Vicario have in prison?**
    A. Diarrhea
    B. He stopped speaking to everyone
    C. Blennorrhea
    D. He fell asleep and wouldn't wake up

11. **Who came up with the solution to both Pedro's blennorrhea and Pablo's problem in # 10?**
    A. Placida Linero
    B. Luisa Santiaga
    C. Pura Vicario
    D. Susana Abdala

12. **According to the narrator, who did most of the townspeople believe to be the only victim?**
    A. Angela Vicario
    B. Santiago Nasar
    C. Bayardo San Roman
    D. the Vicario twins

13. **What did Bayardo San Roman suffer from after he returned Angela?**
    A. A stomach ache
    B. Ethylic Intoxication
    C. A cold
    D. Blennorrhea

14. **How many women came to pick up Bayardo after the wedding?**
    A. 3
    B. 4
    C. 5
    D. 7

15. **What surprised the narrator most when he visited Angela Vicario long after the wedding and murder?**
    A. How young she looked
    B. The way she managed to discuss all of the details of the murder
    C. Her understanding of her life
    D. Her amazing embroidering skills

16. **What event caused Angela to start writing letters to Bayardo?**
    A. A visitor from town mentioned him.
    B. She saw him at the train station.
    C. She read a book about love.
    D. She saw him in a hotel.

17. **What month did Bayardo San Roman finally return to Angela?**
    A. August
    B. January
    C. November
    D. September

18. **How many letters total did Angela write Bayardo?**
    A. Around 500
    B. Around 1,500
    C. Almost 1,000
    D. Almost 2,000

19. What did Cristo Bedoya end up doing with his life?
  A. He married Flora Miguel
  B. He became a well-known surgeon
  C. He became a singer
  D. He took over Santiago's Divine Face farm

20. How many days after the crime did the investigating magistrate show up?
  A. 4 days
  B. 8 days
  C. 12 days
  D. 16 days

21. What alarmed the judge the most about the murder?
  A. The lack of evidence that Santiago had been the cause of wrong against Angela
  B. The bloodthirstiness of the Vicario twins
  C. The fact that no one in town stopped the murder
  D. The general feeling in town that Bayardo was the only victim

22. What did Angela reply when the judge asked her who Santiago Nasar was?
  A. "He was my lover"
  B. "He was my perpetrator"
  C. "He was just a man"
  D. "He stole my honor"

23. What, according to the narrator, was Santiago's reaction when he was told about the murder plot?
  A. "bewilderment of innocence"
  B. "invincibility"
  C. "amusement"
  D. "panic"

24. What did Angela reply when the judge asked her who Santiago Nasar was?
  A. "He was my lover"
  B. "He was my perpetrator"
  C. "He was just a man"
  D. "He stole my honor"

25. **What, according to the narrator, was Santiago's reaction when he was told about the murder plot?**
    A. "bewilderment of innocence"
    B. "invincibility"
    C. "amusement"
    D. "panic"

Quiz 3 Answer Key

1. **(D)** Father Amador
2. **(B)** Dr. Dionisio Iguaran
3. **(C)** "eat his guts"
4. **(B)** Placida Linero
5. **(D)** a gold medal
6. **(C)** A stigma on his right hand
7. **(B)** Hepatitis
8. **(C)** Eating disproportionate amounts of food
9. **(D)** the narrator smelled of Santiago
10. **(A)** Diarrhea
11. **(D)** Susana Abdala
12. **(C)** Bayardo San Roman
13. **(B)** Ethylic Intoxication
14. **(C)** 5
15. **(C)** Her understanding of her life
16. **(D)** She saw him in a hotel.
17. **(A)** August
18. **(D)** Almost 2,000
19. **(B)** He became a well–known surgeon
20. **(C)** 12 days
21. **(A)** The lack of evidence that Santiago had been the cause of wrong against Angela
22. **(B)** "He was my perpetrator"
23. **(A)** "bewilderment of innocence"
24. **(B)** "He was my perpetrator"
25. **(A)** "bewilderment of innocence"

Quiz 4

1. Who did the twins tell of their plot because they thought he was "just the right person to stop the crime without bringing any shame on them"?
   A. Cristo Bedoya
   B. Indalecio Prado
   C. Yamil Shaium
   D. Luis Enrique

2. **Who warned Cristo Bedoya of the murder plot?**
   A. Margot
   B. Luisa Santiaga
   C. Yamil Shaium
   D. Luis Enrique

3. **What did Placida Linero suspect Cristo Bedoya was doing in her son's room?**
   A. Looking for Santiago
   B. Taking a nap
   C. Robbing them
   D. Getting a gun

4. **What did Pedro Vicario call Criso Bedoya when he told him to warn Santiago?**
   A. Cristobal
   B. Cristofer
   C. Cristolin
   D. Cristoson

5. **What did the mayor do instead of taking care of the situation, after Cristo warned him?**
   A. Went inside the social club to check on a date for a dominoes game
   B. Went to visit Maria Cervantes
   C. Went inside the social club to play dominoes
   D. Went home to eat breakfast

6. **Who told Cristo Bedoya that Santiago Nasar had been killed?**
   A. Margot
   B. Luisa Santiaga
   C. Luis Enrique
   D. the Narrator

7. **Who was the wise man of the community?**
    A. Don Rogelio de la Flor
    B. Santiago Nasar
    C. Nahir Miguel
    D. Yamil Shaium

8. **Who was the wise man of the community?**
    A. Don Rogelio de la Flor
    B. Santiago Nasar
    C. Nahir Miguel
    D. Yamil Shaium

9. **What did Flora Miguel return to Santiago when she heard of the murder plot and the motives behind it?**
    A. turquoise earrings
    B. A gold necklace
    C. A chestful of letters
    D. A mother–of–pearl music box

10. **Did Nahir Miguel kick Santiago Nasar out of his house?**
    A. Yes, but he offered him a rifle to protect himself.
    B. N/A
    C. No, he offered him refuge.
    D. Yes.

11. **What did Clotilde Armenta do when the Vicario twins spotted Santiago in the square?**
    A. She grabbed Pablo Vicario and shouted at Santiago to run.
    B. She grabbed Pedro Vicario and shouted at Santiago to run.
    C. She grabbed Pablo Vicario.
    D. She grabbed Pedro Vicario.

12. **Who shut and barred the main door just as Santiago was running up?**
    A. Cristo Bedoya
    B. Placida Linero
    C. Victoria Guzman
    D. Divina Flor

13. **What did Pedro Vicario find unusual about the knife that he used to kill Santiago?**
    A. It looked like it had blood on it even before he attacked Santiago.
    B. It didn't have a drop of blood on it after three stabs.
    C. It felt dull when he attacked Santiago.
    D. It seemed unusually sharp when he attacked Santiago.

14. **How did Santiago Nasar get from the main door, where he was attacked, to his back door?**
    A. He went along the street.
    B. He went around the house.
    C. His mother opened the main door.
    D. He went through a neighbor's house.

15. **Who was the last person Santiago Nasar spoke with?**
    A. Cristo Bedoya
    B. the narrator's mother
    C. the narrator's sister (the nun)
    D. The narrator's aunt

16. **What awoke Pura Vicario when Bayardo came to drop Angela off?**
    A. Three slow knocks on the door
    B. Loud Wailing, from Angela
    C. A feel that something was wrong
    D. The doorbell

17. **Where was Poncio Vicario during the wedding festivities?**
    A. In a chair next to the bride and groom
    B. In bed in the house
    C. On the ground, playing with the children
    D. On a stool, in the middle of the yard

18. **What was wrong with Poncio Vicario?**
    A. He was deaf
    B. He was dumb
    C. He was blind
    D. He was simple

19. **The investigating magistrate thought that it was unfair that "life should make use of so many _____ forbidden literature."**
   A. coincidences
   B. similarities
   C. commonalities
   D. differences

20. **Was the narrator able to use all of the report of the murder for his account?**
   A. No, because he didn't have the patience to find them.
   B. No, because many of the pages were ruined in floods.
   C. No, because the judge was unorganized and lost many pages.
   D. Yes, he read them all.

21. **Where did the twins go to sharpen their knives?**
   A. the blacksmith
   B. the meat market
   C. a friend's house
   D. the stone grinder

22. **How many knives were taken away from the twins before the murder?**
   A. two
   B. none
   C. four
   D. three

23. **Does Clotilde Armenta think that the Vicario twins want to kill Santiago?**
   A. No, she thinks that they want someone to stop them.
   B. Yes, but only because they feel like it's their duty.
   C. No, she thinks they are just drunk and messing around.
   D. Yes, because they have a deep–seated hatred against Santiago because of his wealth.

24. **Does Colonel Aponte detain the twins for a while after taking their knives?**
   A. Yes, but he really just takes them out to breakfast and then to see the bishop.
   B. No, he lets them stay in the milk shop.
   C. Yes, he takes them to the jail for an hour.
   D. No. He sends them home.

25. **Who invited Santiago Nasar to tea, in order to "gain some time to think"?**
    A. Cristo Bedoya
    B. Colonel Aponte
    C. Celeste Dangond
    D. Yamil Shaium

Quiz 4 Answer Key

1. **(B)** Indalecio Prado
2. **(C)** Yamil Shaium
3. **(C)** Robbing them
4. **(A)** Cristobal
5. **(A)** Went inside the social club to check on a date for a dominoes game
6. **(B)** Luisa Santiaga
7. **(C)** Nahir Miguel
8. **(C)** Nahir Miguel
9. **(C)** A chestful of letters
10. **(C)** No, he offered him refuge.
11. **(B)** She grabbed Pedro Vicario and shouted at Santiago to run.
12. **(B)** Placida Linero
13. **(B)** It didn't have a drop of blood on it after three stabs.
14. **(D)** He went through a neighbor's house.
15. **(D)** The narrator's aunt
16. **(A)** Three slow knocks on the door
17. **(D)** On a stool, in the middle of the yard
18. **(C)** He was blind
19. **(A)** coincidences
20. **(B)** No, because many of the pages were ruined in floods.
21. **(B)** the meat market
22. **(A)** two
23. **(A)** No, she thinks that they want someone to stop them.
24. **(D)** No. He sends them home.
25. **(C)** Celeste Dangond

ClassicNotes

GrAdeSaver™

Getting you the grade since 1999™

Other ClassicNotes from GradeSaver™

1984
Absalom, Absalom
Adam Bede
The Adventures of Augie March
The Adventures of Huckleberry Finn
The Adventures of Tom Sawyer
The Aeneid
Agamemnon
The Age of Innocence
Alice in Wonderland
All My Sons
All Quiet on the Western Front
All the King's Men
All the Pretty Horses
The Ambassadors
American Beauty
Angela's Ashes
Animal Farm
Anna Karenina
Antigone
Antony and Cleopatra
Aristotle's Ethics
Aristotle's Poetics
Aristotle's Politics
As I Lay Dying
As You Like It
The Awakening
Babbitt
The Bacchae
Bartleby the Scrivener
The Bean Trees
The Bell Jar

Beloved
Benito Cereno
Beowulf
Billy Budd
Black Boy
Bluest Eye
Brave New World
Breakfast at Tiffany's
Call of the Wild
Candide
The Canterbury Tales
Cat's Cradle
Catch-22
The Catcher in the Rye
The Caucasian Chalk Circle
The Cherry Orchard
The Chosen
A Christmas Carol
Chronicle of a Death Foretold
Civil Disobedience
Civilization and Its Discontents
A Clockwork Orange
The Color of Water
The Color Purple
Comedy of Errors
Communist Manifesto
A Confederacy of Dunces
Connecticut Yankee in King Arthur's Court
Coriolanus
The Count of Monte Cristo

Crime and Punishment
The Crucible
Cry, the Beloved Country
The Crying of Lot 49
Cymbeline
Daisy Miller
Death in Venice
Death of a Salesman
The Death of Ivan Ilych
Democracy in America
Devil in a Blue Dress
The Diary of Anne Frank
Disgrace
Divine Comedy-I: Inferno
A Doll's House
Don Quixote Book I
Don Quixote Book II
Dr. Faustus
Dr. Jekyll and Mr. Hyde
Dracula
Dubliners
East of Eden
Emma
Endgame
Ethan Frome
The Eumenides
Everything is Illuminated
Fahrenheit 451
The Fall of the House of Usher
Farewell to Arms
The Federalist Papers
For Whom the Bell Tolls
The Fountainhead

For our full list of over 250 Study Guides, Quizzes,
Sample College Application Essays, Literature Essays and E-texts, visit:

www.gradesaver.com

ClassicNotes

GrAdeSaver™

Getting you the grade since 1999™

Other ClassicNotes from GradeSaver™

Frankenstein
Franny and Zooey
Glass Menagerie
The God of Small Things
The Grapes of Wrath
Great Expectations
The Great Gatsby
Hamlet
The Handmaid's Tale
Hard Times
Heart of Darkness
Hedda Gabler
Henry IV (Pirandello)
Henry IV Part 1
Henry IV Part 2
Henry V
The Hobbit
Homo Faber
House of Mirth
House of the Seven
    Gables
House on Mango Street
Howards End
A Hunger Artist
I Know Why the Caged
    Bird Sings
An Ideal Husband
Iliad
The Importance of Being
    Earnest
In Our Time
Inherit the Wind
Invisible Man
The Island of Dr. Moreau
Jane Eyre
Jazz

The Joy Luck Club
Julius Caesar
Jungle of Cities
Kidnapped
King Lear
Last of the Mohicans
Leviathan
Libation Bearers
The Lion, the Witch and
    the Wardrobe
Lolita
Long Day's Journey Into
    Night
Lord Jim
Lord of the Flies
The Lord of the Rings:
    The Fellowship of the
    Ring
The Lord of the Rings:
    The Return of the
    King
The Lord of the Rings:
    The Two Towers
A Lost Lady
The Love Song of J.
    Alfred Prufrock
Lucy
Macbeth
Madame Bovary
Manhattan Transfer
Mansfield Park
The Mayor of
    Casterbridge
Measure for Measure
Medea
Merchant of Venice

Metamorphoses
The Metamorphosis
Middlemarch
Midsummer Night's
    Dream
Moby Dick
Moll Flanders
Mother Courage and Her
    Children
Mrs. Dalloway
Much Ado About
    Nothing
My Antonia
Native Son
Night
No Exit
Notes from Underground
O Pioneers
The Odyssey
Oedipus Rex / Oedipus
    the King
Of Mice and Men
The Old Man and the Sea
On Liberty
One Day in the Life of
    Ivan Denisovich
One Flew Over the
    Cuckoo's Nest
One Hundred Years of
    Solitude
Oroonoko
Othello
Our Town
Pale Fire
Paradise Lost
A Passage to India

For our full list of over 250 Study Guides, Quizzes,
Sample College Application Essays, Literature Essays and E-texts, visit:

www.gradesaver.com

ClassicNotes

GrAdeSaver™

Getting you the grade since 1999™

Other ClassicNotes from GradeSaver™

The Pearl
The Picture of Dorian Gray
Poems of W.B. Yeats: The Rose
Portrait of the Artist as a Young Man
Pride and Prejudice
Prometheus Bound
Pudd'nhead Wilson
Pygmalion
Rabbit, Run
A Raisin in the Sun
Red Badge of Courage
The Republic
Richard II
Richard III
The Rime of the Ancient Mariner
Robinson Crusoe
Roll of Thunder, Hear My Cry
Romeo and Juliet
A Room of One's Own
A Room With a View
Rosencrantz and Guildenstern Are Dead
Salome
The Scarlet Letter
Secret Sharer
Sense and Sensibility
A Separate Peace
Shakespeare's Sonnets
Siddhartha
Silas Marner

Sir Gawain and the Green Knight
Sister Carrie
Six Characters in Search of an Author
Slaughterhouse Five
Snow Falling on Cedars
Something Wicked This Way Comes
Song of Roland
Sons and Lovers
The Sorrows of Young Werther
The Sound and the Fury
Spring Awakening
The Stranger
A Streetcar Named Desire
The Sun Also Rises
Tale of Two Cities
The Taming of the Shrew
The Tempest
Tender is the Night
Tess of the D'Urbervilles
Their Eyes Were Watching God
Things Fall Apart
The Threepenny Opera
The Time Machine
Titus Andronicus
To Build a Fire
To Kill a Mockingbird
To the Lighthouse
Treasure Island
Troilus and Cressida
Turn of the Screw

Twelfth Night
Ulysses
Uncle Tom's Cabin
Utopia
A Very Old Man With Enormous Wings
The Visit
Volpone
Waiting for Godot
Waiting for Lefty
Walden
Washington Square
Where the Red Fern Grows
White Fang
White Noise
White Teeth
Who's Afraid of Virginia Woolf
Winesburg, Ohio
The Winter's Tale
Woyzeck
Wuthering Heights
The Yellow Wallpaper
Yonnondio: From the Thirties

For our full list of over 250 Study Guides, Quizzes,
Sample College Application Essays, Literature Essays and E-texts, visit:

www.gradesaver.com

Made in the USA
Lexington, KY
27 March 2013